Lala Salama

An African Lullaby in Swahili and English

For Muth and Fath, with love

Lala Salama

HANNAH HERITAGE BOZYLINSKY

Philomel Books

Lala salama
Twiga
Mwewe

Peace, sleep well
Giraffe
Hawk

Lala salama
Nyani
Nungu

Peace, sleep well
Baboon
Porcupine

Lala salama
Fisi
Sungura

Peace, sleep well
Hyena
Hare

Ndege
Kifaru!
Lala salama

Birds
Rhinoceros!
Peace, sleep well

Salama
Swala granti

Peace
Gazelle

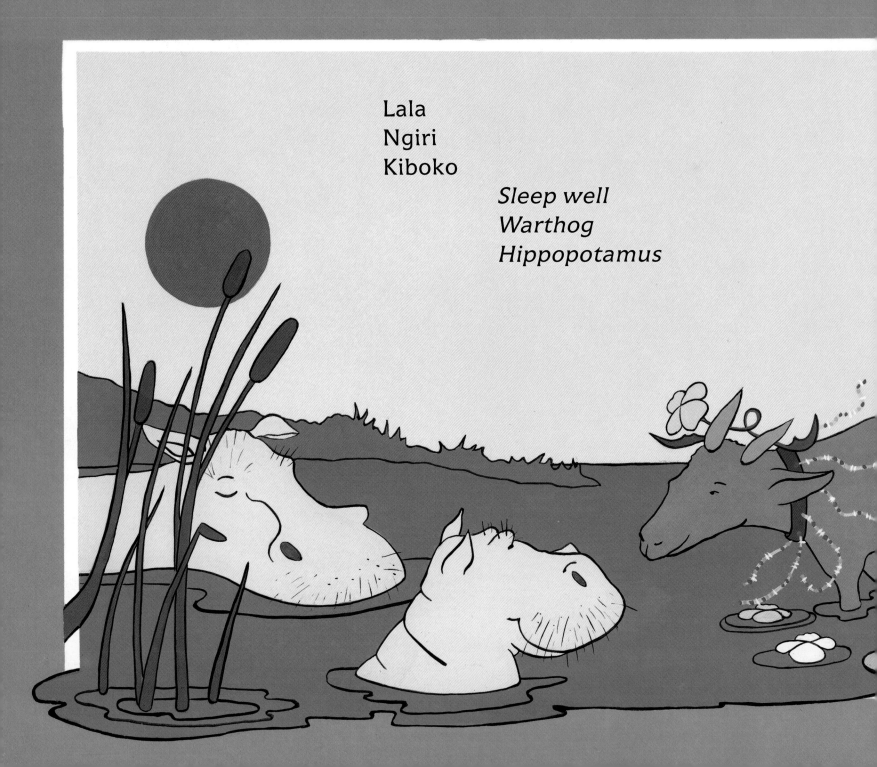

Lala
Ngiri
Kiboko

Sleep well
Warthog
Hippopotamus

Lala salama
Tembo
Nyoka

Peace, sleep well
Elephant
Snake

Mamba!
Bweha

Crocodile!
Jackal

Simba
Nyati

Lion
Buffalo

Salama
Punda Milia
Lala salama

Peace
Zebra
Peace, sleep well

Ng'ombe
Mbuzi

Cattle
Goat

Mama, Mama,
Lala salama

Mama, Mama
Peace, sleep well

Lala salama

Peace, sleep well

AUTHOR'S NOTE

For many Masai, daily life has changed little during the past one thousand years. Masai boys still herd the family's cattle and goats, sometimes walking miles into the wild savanna in search of food and water. Their only protection is a walking stick or a small club. A Masai boy does not know how many cattle or goats his family owns because it is bad luck to count them. However, he can still tell at a glance if one has wandered or been carried off by a hyena or a lion.

Masai girls help their mothers at home by caring for the younger children and babies. They also repair the *boma*, or hut, with a mixture of mud and cattle dung that they rub onto its roof and walls.

At the end of the day, the family will drink a mixture of cattle blood and milk which is stored in gourds decorated with leather and beads. This drink is a large part of the Masai diet.

While visiting the Masai, I found that their simple lifestyle, their respect and love of the natural world, and the beautiful language of East Africa made them the perfect subject for this African lullaby.

—*Hannah Heritage Bozylinsky*

PRONUNCIATION KEY

la la salama	LA' - la sa - LA' - ma	kiboko	kee - BO' - ko
twiga	TWEE' - ga	tembo	TEM'- bo
mwewe	m - WEH' - weh	nyoka	n - YO' - ka
nyani	n - YA' - nee	mamba	MAM' - ba
nungu	NOON'- goo	bweha	BWEH' - ha
fisi	FEE' - see	simba	SIM'- ba
sungura	SOON' - goo - ra	nyati	n -YA' - tee
ndege	n - DEH'- geh	punda milia	POON' - da meh - LEE' - ya
kifaru	kee - FA' - roo	ng'ombe	n - GOM' - beh
swala granti	SWA'- la gran - TEE'	mbuzi	m - BOO' - zee
ngiri	n - GEE'- ree		

This pronunciation key has been developed with assistance by Lea Masiello, Ph.D., Director of the Writing Center, Indiana University of Pennsylvania, and Nourou Yakoubou, graduate student in linguistics from Togo, Africa. Several words have different pronunciations according to local dialects; pronunciations were selected that were most common to Tanzania, home of the Masai.

Copyright © 1993 by Hannah Heritage Bozylinsky. Published by Philomel Books, a division of The Putnam & Grosset Group, 200 Madison Avenue, New York, NY 10016. All rights reserved. This book, or parts thereof, may not be reproduced in any form without permission in writing from the publisher. Published simultaneously in Canada. Printed in Hong Kong by South China Printing Co., (1988) Ltd. Book design by Gunta Alexander. The text is set in Icone. Library of Congress Cataloging-in-Publication Data Bozylinsky, Hannah Heritage. Lala salama / Hannah Heritage Bozylinsky. p. cm. English and Swahili. Summary: An African lullaby in Swahili and English in which a little boy says good night to all the animals and ends with his mother. [1. Bedtime—Poetry. 2. Animals—Poetry. 3. Africa—Poetry. 4. Lullabies. 5. Swahili language materials—Bilingual.] I. Title. PZ90.S94B68 1993 896 .3921—dc20 92-23028 CIP AC ISBN 0-399-22022-4

1 3 5 7 9 10 8 6 4 2

First Impression